Tails from the Trail:

The HILARIOUS CHRONICLES of DOG WALKING

Shaun Marshall

ACKNOWLEDGEMENTS

Barry and Rosie,

Glenys and Dottie,

Martika and Bear,

Barbara and Pedro,

Peter and his pack, including Raith

Thankyou for all your time, suffering, listening to me and my wild crazy ideas, and of course, the spare poo bags!!

TABLE OF CONTENTS

INTRODUCTION:

Welcome to the Pack

If you've ever walked a dog, you already know: it's never just a walk. A simple trip to the park can turn into an unexpected social gathering, a game of detective work when your dog decides to roll in something foul, or a full-body workout as you chase them down after they spot a squirrel.

Dog walking is a daily adventure, a ritual filled with unpredictability, laughter, and the occasional chaos. It's a world where strangers become familiar, where conversations revolve around the weather and the best local pet-friendly cafés, and where our four-legged companions often make the rules.

In this book, we'll explore the hilarious, sometimes absurd, always entertaining world of dog walking. Whether it's the perils of summer strolls, the soggy misadventures of rainy-day walks, or the unspoken etiquette of finding a lost ball, every outing has a story.

So, leash up, lace up your mud-proof boots, and let's step into the life of a dog walker, where the dogs are in charge, and we're just along for the ride.

CHAPTER 1:

The Summer Walk Struggle

Before I start, my dog is called 7, a beautiful black and white springer spaniel—'a rescue dog,' a puppy when I found her.

Summer dog walks sound lovely, in theory. You picture yourself strolling through sun-dappled fields, your dog happily trotting beside you, maybe even a gentle breeze to keep things cool.

In reality?

It's a sweaty endurance test featuring melted tarmac, panting dogs, and the overwhelming scent of wet fur when your dog inevitably finds the only muddy puddle in a five-mile radius.

And if you have a dog like 7, the adventure level increases.

She has two essential requirements for every single walk: a ball or a stick. Or, ideally, both.

She is a firm believer in the 'one in the mouth, one in the paws' method, and if she has to carry an entire tree branch alongside her favorite tennis ball, so be it. There is no such thing as too many items to carry—only weak humans who don't understand the importance of multitasking.

Of course, once she has her prized possessions, getting her to let go of them is another challenge entirely.

THE 'TOO HOT TO WALK' DEBATE

Dog walkers have an unspoken summer routine: checking the temperature at least seven times before leaving the house. Anything above 20°C (68°F) sets off a moral dilemma.

Too hot? Just warm? Will the pavement burn their paws? Should I go barefoot outside to check? And if it's too hot now, should I wake up at an unholy hour tomorrow to walk them at dawn?

Of course, there are always those over-enthusiastic dogs who refuse to acknowledge the heat. While their owners practically melt, these dogs sprint full speed across the park like it's the doggy Olympics.

Then there are the dramatic ones—the moment they step outside and feel the heat, they collapse like they've been shot, refusing to move until carried home.

And then there's me, standing in the middle of the park, attempting to explain to my dog that, *yes, we do have to go home now because it's too hot.* And no, flopping onto the grass in protest does not count as a reasonable counter-argument.

THE WATER BOTTLE PROBLEM

No matter how prepared you think you are, you're never quite ready.

Either you forget the water bottle, or you bring one and your dog refuses to drink from it, insisting that the murky puddle on the path is much tastier.

And if you do remember the water, you'll soon discover the universal rule of dog walking:

✓ The more expensive the portable water bowl, the less your dog wants to drink from it.

7 never drank from my specially chosen bottle but from everyone else's.

You could buy the latest, state-of-the-art, collapsible, ergonomic, BPA-free dog bowl, and they'll still choose a muddy puddle, a lake, or a random discarded cup at the park.

THE GREAT SUMMER STICK BATTLE

Dogs love sticks, but in summer, they take it to another level.

Every walk turns into a treasure hunt, where they scour the ground for the biggest, most impractical tree branch they can possibly carry.

Size doesn't matter—your tiny Chihuahua will attempt to drag a log twice their size, while your Labrador insists on running full speed with a branch so wide it clotheslines everyone in its path.

And let's not forget the inevitable stick disputes.

Your dog finds the perfect stick, only for another dog to also claim it. Now you're standing awkwardly while two dogs engage in an intense tug-of-war, neither willing to back down.

The other owner and I exchange a polite smile while silently wondering: *Who will break first— the dogs or us?*

THE 'WHY IS MY DOG WET?' MYSTERY

It's 30 degrees outside. The ground is dry. There's no visible water source in sight.

So why, for the love of all things good, is my dog soaking wet?

Dogs have a magical ability to find water where there shouldn't be any.

A hidden puddle, a swampy ditch, someone's unattended garden sprinkler—whatever it is, they will find it.

And roll in it.

And look so pleased with themselves afterward.

THE 'JUST A QUICK WALK' LIE

Every dog owner has, at some point, uttered the words, "Just a quick walk today."

This is a lie.

There is no such thing as a quick walk.

A 'quick' stroll always turns into a 45-minute trek because:

✓ Your dog refuses to leave the park.

✓ You run into someone you haven't seen in months and need to catch up.

✓ Your dog makes a new friend, and you now feel obligated to stay.

✓ You take a different route and end up somewhere completely unexpected.

By the time you get home, both you and your dog are exhausted, overheated, and somehow still covered in mud, despite there being no mud in sight.

FINAL THOUGHTS ON SUMMER WALKS

Summer walks are a battle of endurance, hydration, and trying to convince your dog that they don't need to carry that massive stick home.

They're sweaty, chaotic, and occasionally frustrating but also full of unexpected joy—watching dogs play in the sunshine, finding the perfect shady spot under a tree, and the unspoken camaraderie of fellow overheated dog owners.

And as soon as summer ends?

We'll all be complaining that it's too cold.

CHAPTER 2:

Rainy Walks—Wet Dogs,
Wet People, and Lost Shoes

If summer walks are about sweat, sunburn, and overheating, then rainy walks are about embracing chaos. Because no matter how much you check the forecast, no matter how prepared you think you are, one universal truth remains: *if you own a dog, you will get caught in the rain.*

And it won't be a light drizzle. Oh no. It will be the kind of rain that turns the pavement into a river, soaks you to your socks in under five seconds, and makes you question every decision that led you to this moment.

THE FIVE STAGES OF RAIN WALK DENIAL

Before the walk even begins, every dog owner goes through the same emotional journey when they realize it might rain:

1. Optimism: "It probably won't rain. The forecast says only a 30% chance!"

2. Doubt: "Well… 30% isn't nothing. But maybe it'll pass."

3. Denial: "It's fine. I'll be quick. We'll be back before it starts."

4. Regret: "Cue downpour the moment you step outside."

5. Acceptance: "Well, we live here now, might as well embrace it."

Meanwhile, your dog has one of two reactions:

- Type A: The Enthusiast—This dog loves the rain. They dive headfirst into puddles, sprint around like lunatics, and seem genuinely offended when you try to take them home.

- Type B: The Drama Queen—The moment they feel a single drop of rain, they act like they've been personally betrayed. They freeze. They glare at you. They refuse to move.

If you own a *Drama Queen* dog, congratulations: you're now the person standing in the rain, trying to convince a 20-pound fluffball that they must walk because they refused to poop in the garden earlier.

PUDDLE ROULETTE: WILL THEY OR WON'T THEY?

Puddles are an unavoidable feature of rainy dog walks. The only question is: how will your dog react?

1. The Puddle Jumper: Leaps in like it's the Olympic long jump, splashing water in all directions, including onto you.

2. The Puddle Snob: Tiptoes around every puddle like they're too good for them, acting like they can't possibly get their paws wet.

3. The Puddle Roller: Finds the absolute dirtiest puddle and rolls in it with the enthusiasm of a pig in mud.

4. The Puddle Drinker: Ignores the fresh, clean water you brought and insists on lapping up murky puddle water instead.

By the end of the walk, even if you tried to avoid puddles, your dog will be wet and muddy and will shake themselves off the moment you step into the house.

THE "OH NO, WHERE'S MY SHOE?" INCIDENT

Rainy walks are when you discover just how badly your shoes handle water. No matter what you're wearing, the moment you step in deep mud, there is a high chance your shoe will get sucked off your foot like a sacrifice to the rain gods.

And if you're extra lucky, this will happen in front of another dog walker. Nothing humbles you faster than trying to dig your shoe out of a mud pit while your dog enthusiastically pulls in the opposite direction.

RAINY DAY CONVERSATIONS: SHARED SUFFERING

When two dog walkers cross paths in the rain, the conversation is less about the weather and more about shared survival.

- "Thought I could beat the rain. I was wrong."
- "Why do we even bother with towels? He's just gonna shake mud everywhere anyway."
- "Might as well let them get as muddy as they want now. No point fighting it."
- "Do you think if we just let them outside, they'd walk themselves?"

There's a special camaraderie among those caught in a downpour with their dogs. We don't judge. We simply nod, accept our mutual fate, and trudge on.

POST-WALK: THE TOWEL BATTLE

The walk might be over, but the real challenge is just beginning: drying your dog before they can turn your house into a crime scene of muddy paw prints.

Again, my friend, Helen, has a military-style operation of how to re-enter the home. It's too long to explain here, but I'm sure you have a similar arrangement.

- Step 1: Attempt to towel them off.
- Step 2: They break free and do the forbidden full-body shake, soaking everything in a five-foot radius.

- Step 3: They sprint around the house in chaotic circles, somehow getting muddier despite the fact that the walk is over.
- Step 4: Accept your fate. The house will be damp forever now.

FINAL THOUGHTS ON RAIN WALKS

Rainy walks are not for the weak. They require patience, waterproof clothing, and the ability to laugh when your dog belly-flops into a puddle. They're messy, frustrating, and completely unavoidable.

But somehow, despite the chaos, there's something oddly enjoyable about them. Maybe it's the way dogs embrace the rain without a second thought. Maybe it's the shared suffering between dog walkers. Or maybe it's the fact that, at the end of it all, there's nothing cosier than drying off and curling up with a damp, tired dog who—despite it all—still thinks you're the best human ever.

And then, just as you've finally dried off, you hear that unmistakable sound:

The dog shake.

And you know it's all about to start again.

CHAPTER 3:

Big Dogs vs. Little Dogs—A Size Debate!

There are two kinds of dog walkers in this world: those walking big dogs and those walking little dogs. And while we all belong to the same dog-loving community, the differences between the two groups are impossible to ignore.

Big dog owners? They're constantly being pulled like human sledges. Little dog owners? They're stopping every two minutes because their dog has opinions about which way to go.

One thing is certain: no matter which size you have, you will always be amazed at how different their behaviour is.

BIG DOGS: THE GENTLE GIANTS (WHO FORGET THEIR SIZE)

Big dogs operate under one major flaw: they do not believe they are big. You can have a 100-pound German Shepherd, and they will still try to climb onto your lap like a tiny Chihuahua.

BIG DOG ENERGY INCLUDES:

- Trying to sit in a café chair like a person.
- Lying across an entire park bench as if they own it.
- Knocking over furniture (and people) with their tails.

- Thinking they can fit in a tiny dog bed and looking confused when they don't.

A walk with a big dog is never a leisurely stroll. It is either a power walk or a full sprint, depending on what they've spotted in the distance. And if they see a squirrel? You'd better hope your shoes have a good grip because you're going with them.

And yet, despite their size and strength, big dogs are some of the biggest scaredy-cats on the planet.

- A leaf blows across the pavement? Immediate panic.

- A small dog barks at them? Complete emotional devastation.

- They step in something squishy? Existential crisis.

No one ever expects the giant dog to be the wimpiest one in the group, yet here we are.

LITTLE DOGS: TINY BUT FIERCE

If big dogs don't know their size, little dogs refuse to acknowledge theirs. They walk through life with the confidence of a wolf pack leader, completely unaware that they weigh less than a sack of flour.

LITTLE DOG ENERGY INCLUDES:

- Barking at dogs 20 times their size.

- Thinking they own every park, café, and street they walk on.

- Getting away with absolute nonsense because they're small and cute.

- Fitting in tiny spaces and scaring their owners when they disappear.

The funniest part? Little dogs control the big dogs.

A tiny terrier will charge straight at a Great Dane, barking like an angry gremlin, and the Great Dane will immediately be like, *'Oh no, a terrifying creature! Must avoid at all costs!'*

Meanwhile, the little dog owner is just standing there, apologising:

"Sorry, he thinks he's a Rottweiler, and his name is Tyson."

Walking a little dog comes with its own set of problems, though. Unlike big dogs—who can charge through anything—little dogs are fussy.

- "This pavement feels weird. I'm not walking."

- "I've decided I don't like this street. Let's turn around."

- "You expect me to walk through wet grass?

- In THESE paws? Absolutely not."

At some point, every small dog owner has given up and just picked their dog up for the rest of the walk. It's the price we pay for having a doggie dictator.

THE MEETING: WHEN BIG DOG AND LITTLE DOG CROSS PATHS

When a big dog and a little dog meet on a walk, it can go one of three ways:

1. Instant Best Friends: They sniff each other, tails wag, and suddenly, they're playing like they've known each other for years.

2. The 'I Don't See You' Approach: One of them (usually the big dog) pretends the other doesn't exist to avoid social awkwardness.

3. The Standoff: The little dog growls, the big dog looks confused, and both owners stand there awkwardly, pretending their dogs are totally normal.

Regardless of how it goes, one thing remains constant: everyone in the park is watching because no one can resist a size-difference dog duo.

FINAL THOUGHTS ON BIG VS. LITTLE DOGS

At the end of the day, whether your dog is the size of a horse or fits in a handbag, they all have one thing in common: they make our walks infinitely more entertaining.

Big dogs keep us humble by proving we are not in control.

Little dogs keep us on our toes by refusing to follow instructions.

And both of them? Love us unconditionally— no matter how ridiculous we look trying to keep up with them.

Do you let your dog on the bed? Of course, we do, or,at least I do.

A total dead weight never moves unless pushed, and amazingly takes up so much room on the bed even the smallest dogs become like lead weights if you need them to move.

CHAPTER 4:

Conversations on the Trail—
The Weather, The Plans, The Hot Gossip

Dog walking isn't just about getting exercise or letting our four-legged friends stretch their legs. It's also about talking to other people who are equally as obsessed with their dogs as we are.

The moment you start walking a dog regularly, you become part of an unspoken social club—a network of people whose interactions follow very specific, time-honoured traditions.

THE WEATHER REPORT: A DOG WALKER'S FAVORITE TOPIC

If there is one thing dog walkers love discussing, it's the weather.

It doesn't matter how many times we've checked the forecast before leaving the house—we must verbally confirm our weather opinions with other walkers we meet.

Common Dog Walker Weather Phrases:

- "Bit chilly this morning, isn't it?"

- "At least the rain held off!"

- "I thought it was going to be warmer than this."

- "Supposed to rain later—better get this walk in while we can!"

- "They say we're in for a heatwave next week!"in England were always talking about the weather.

These conversations can last anywhere from thirty seconds (a quick passing comment) to ten minutes (a full weather analysis, complete with dramatic sighs about how unpredictable it is).

And if you walk the same route every day? You will have this exact conversation with the same people every single morning.

THE "WE SHOULD GO FOR A GROUP WALK" LIE

Every dog walker has at least one acquaintance they see regularly—the 'familiar face' friend.

You don't know much about them beyond their dog's name and the fact that you always run into each other at the park. You chat, you laugh, you part ways…and every now and then, one of you says:

"We should do a proper walk together one day!"

And then? It never happens.

It's not that either of you don't want to. It's just that dog-walking friendships exist in a very specific space we talk when we see each other, but we don't actually plan anything.

And honestly? That's okay. There's something beautiful about these little, casual friendships—where you might never know each other's actual names, but you'll always remember their dog's name.

THE PARK GOSSIP NETWORK

Think small towns have the best gossip? Try a popular dog-walking route.

If you've been walking in the same park for a while, you probably know:

- Which dogs are 'troublemakers.'

- Who refuses to pick up after their dog.

- Which dog is a serial ball thief.

- Which owners have weird opinions on dog training.

- Has he even got a poo bag? Women always have a pocket full!

And if you don't know? Give it time—someone will tell you.

Dog walkers love to swap stories, and once you're part of the community, you will inevitably find yourself in the know.

THE BALL DILEMMA: LOST, FOUND, STOLEN

Every dog owner has, at some point, lost a ball.

Every dog owner has also, at some point, found a random ball that doesn't belong to them.

And thus, the great unspoken ball economy of dog walking begins.

The Four Types of Ball Situations:

1. The Honest Retrieval: You see a lost ball, pick it up, and try to return it to the rightful owner.

2. The Accidental Adoption: Your dog finds a ball and refuses to give it up. You spend the next ten minutes apologiseing to the other owner while trying (and failing) to swap it for their original one.

3. The 'Finders Keepers' Debate: A ball is lying abandoned in the grass. You hesitate. Has someone lost it? Is it fair game now? Do you take it, or is there an unwritten rule against it?

4. The Mystery Ball: You arrive home and realise your dog somehow acquired a ball you don't remember them picking up.

The unofficial rule seems to be: if it's clearly a dog's favourite ball, give it back. If it looks abandoned, it's fair game. If no one claims it? Congratulations, your dog just won the lottery.

FINAL THOUGHTS ON DOG WALKER CONVERSATIONS

Dog walking is more than just a daily routine. It's a social experience, a community, and sometimes, even a source of entertainment.

Whether we're complaining about the weather, gossiping about a misbehaving dog, or engaging in the eternal ball trade, one thing is certain:

We might be walking our dogs, but in the process, we're building connections—one random chat at a time or just talking to ourselves, that's where we find all the right answers.

CHAPTER 5:

Why Is It Mostly Women Walking Dogs?

If you've spent any time at a park, on a beach, or walking in the woods with your dog, you've probably noticed something: *Most dog walkers are women.*

Sure, you'll see the occasional man with a leash in hand, but in general, the dog-walking community is heavily female-dominated.

Why?

The theories are endless, but after years of observation, I've narrowed it down to a few key reasons.

THEORY #1: WOMEN ARE THE DEFAULT CAREGIVERS

Let's be real—whether it's kids, pets, or plants, women often end up being the ones responsible for keeping things alive.

You could have a couple who both agree they want a dog, but somehow, after they get the dog, the daily walks become her job.

✓ "Oh, I'd love to walk the dog, but I have work."
(So do I.)

✓ "You do such a good job with them!"
(Great, thanks, I guess?)

✓ "I'll take them out later." (Spoiler: No, you won't.)

This is not to say men never walk the dog. Of course they do! But let's be honest—when you do see a man out walking a dog, it's often because:

1. His partner is sick or busy.

2. He's been specifically instructed to do so.

3. It's a really, really big dog, and he enjoys the sense of strength that comes with it.

Which brings us to…

THEORY #2: MEN ONLY SEEM TO WALK CERTAIN TYPES OF DOGS

If you were to line up all the dog-walking men you see, I guarantee you'd start to notice a pattern:

Men tend to walk BIG dogs.

If you see a guy with a dog, it's usually a:

✓ German Shepherd

✓ Husky

✓ Labrador Retriever

✓ Rottweiler

✔ Any dog that looks like it might have been in a police K9 unit

Meanwhile, the smaller, fluffier dogs? Almost always walked by women.

It's as if men have collectively decided: "If I'm going to be seen in public with a dog, it has to look tough."

Meanwhile, women? They walk everything.

✔ Big dogs

✔ Small dogs

✔ Overly enthusiastic spaniels that don't know how to stop bouncing.

They don't discriminate. They just put on their walking shoes and get on with it.

THEORY #3: WOMEN ACTUALLY ENJOY THE SOCIAL SIDE OF DOG WALKING

Dog walking isn't just about exercise—it's also a social activity, listening to audiobooks, and just a space for themselves.

Women are much more likely to:

✔ Stop and chat with another dog owner.

✓ Remember the names of dogs they see regularly.

✓ Exchange numbers for future 'doggy playdates.'

✓ Offer advice about the best local dog-friendly cafes.

Men? Not so much.

If a guy is walking a dog alone, he usually follows one of three approaches:

1. The Head Nod & Move On: He acknowledges you just enough to be polite, then keeps walking.

2. The Quick Compliment: "Nice dog." Then immediately leaves.

3. The 'I Was Forced Into This' Look: He's walking the dog, but you can tell he's on a mission to get it done as fast as possible.

This is why, if you go to any park, you'll see groups of women chatting away while the men just...wander around, throwing a ball in silence.

THEORY #4: WOMEN KNOW ALL THE DOG-FRIENDLY SPOTS

Women are the planners when it comes to dog-friendly locations.

Ask a woman where she walks her dog, and she'll give you a detailed list of:

✓ The best parks, beaches, or woodland trails.

✓ Which cafes allow dogs inside.

✓ The best walking routes that aren't muddy.

✓ Which local pubs and cafes give out dog treats.

✓ The places where 'people don't pick up after their dogs, so avoid that bit.'

Ask a man where he walks his dog, and he'll say:

"Uh…the park?"

THEORY #5: WOMEN JUST HAVE MORE PATIENCE

Men often underestimate how much patience it takes to walk a dog.

✓ When a dog refuses to move because they're sniffing something very important, a woman waits. A man sighs loudly and tries to pull them away.

✓ When a dog meets another dog and they start playing, a woman enjoys the moment. A man checks his watch like he has somewhere better to be.

✓ When a dog rolls in something disgusting, a woman swears but gets out the baby wipes. A man goes straight to: "That's it—we're going home."

Women accept the chaos of dog walking.

Men? They endure it.

THE RIGHT CLOTHES FOR THE JOB (AND WHY MEN NEVER HAVE THEM)

Women understand that dog walking requires proper clothing.

Take my amazing friend, Helen, for example.

Helen treats walking her two dogs like a military operation—meticulously planned and highly organised. She has long legs, so it's on the verge of a March, absolutely not for the faint-hearted.

Her dogs? Always are off chasing deer, staring at their own reflections in puddles, or chasing balls.

Her approach to planning a walk? Miles and miles of pure endurance.

For Helen, it's not just a walk—it's a hike, a flask of tea and cake in the backpack, or even a rendezvous at a cafe or any pub before the return assault.

And she does it in any weather.

Helen's philosophy is simple: "It's never too cold if you have the right clothes on."

And, annoyingly…she's right.

She's always fully prepared, wrapped up in her bright pink dog-walking coat (which, honestly, she looks fantastic in—you can never lose her in a crowd). Add in the bobble hat, the bag of essentials (poo bags, chocolate, and who knows what else), and she's ready for anything.

Meanwhile, men?

They never dress properly.

Women are bundled up in waterproofs, thermal socks, gloves, and sturdy boots.

Men? They're out there freezing, unprepared, and usually in a hurry to go home.

And me? I never have the right shoes, and my coat is not waterproof anymore.

Every single time, without fail, I end up with wet feet. You'd think I'd learn, but somehow, I don't. I must go through three pairs of trainers each winter, just to look cool!

Oh, and pet shops? A money drain, or is that just a man thing?

You go in for one thing, and somehow, you leave with five new chews, a fancy collar, and the latest squeaky toy. Because let's be honest—there's no such thing as not spoiling your best friend.

FINAL THOUGHTS ON THE DOG WALKING GENDER DIVIDE

Does this mean men never walk dogs? Of course not.

But if you ever find yourself wondering, "Why do I mostly see women out here?" Well, now you know.

It's because women are the organisers, the social ones, the caregivers, the planners, and—most importantly—the ones who don't mind standing in the rain while their dog refuses to pee.

Because that takes a special kind of patience. Women are special in so many ways.

CHAPTER 6:

Dogs in Shops, Cafés, and Other Unexpected Places

For years, dogs were strictly 'outdoor animals' when it came to public spaces. You could walk them in the park, you could take them on the beach (sometimes), but the moment you tried to step inside a shop or café, you'd be met with *the look*.

You know the one. The *'Absolutely not, get that beast out of here immediately'* look.

But times have changed, and now, more and more places are opening their doors to our four-legged friends. Dog-friendly cafes, pubs, and even shops are popping up everywhere. And while this is fantastic for dog lovers, it has also introduced a whole new level of social confusion.

THE THRILL OF FINDING A DOG-FRIENDLY CAFE

Few things bring a dog walker as much joy as discovering a café where dogs are allowed inside.

The first time you see the little 'Dogs Welcome' sign on the door, it feels like unlocking a secret level in life.

- "You mean I don't have to sit outside in the freezing cold?"

- "I can drink my coffee without awkwardly tying my dog to a chair and hoping they don't drag it across the pavement?"

- "There are FREE treats at the counter??"

It's a magical moment.

And once you find one dog-friendly café, you go on a mission to find them all.

THE SLIGHTLY AWKWARD PROCESS OF BRINGING YOUR DOG INSIDE

Of course, just because a place allows dogs doesn't mean every dog knows how to behave inside a café.

Some dogs enter like polite, well-mannered citizens. They sit nicely under the table, they wait patiently, and they don't make a sound.

Others? Absolute chaos. .

- Barking at the coffee machine because it makes a weird noise.

- Refusing to settle, so you spend the entire time awkwardly repositioning them.

- Begging. So much begging.

- Deciding that now is the perfect time to start rolling on the floor for no reason.

And if you have a big dog? Forget personal space. That Labrador will wedge themselves between two tables, knocking over at least one chair in the process.

But no matter how awkward it gets, one thing remains true:

We will always go back. Because once you've had a coffee indoors with your dog beside you, there's no turning back.

SHOPS: THE GREAT DOG-WELCOMING MYSTERY

Unlike cafés, where rules are (usually) clear, shops are a complete gamble.

Some stores welcome dogs with open arms, even providing biscuits at the counter. Others? They act like you've just walked in with a live goat.

The tricky part? There's often no sign.

This leads to the awkward moment where you hesitate at the entrance, trying to:

✓ Spot any other dogs inside.

✓ Make eye contact with an employee for some kind of unspoken approval.

✓ Pretend to read a product label while actually waiting to see if anyone kicks you out.

And sometimes, you think it's fine...until it isn't.

- "Sorry, no dogs in here."

- Cue the shameful retreat as you apologise profusely and leave.

The best-case scenario? You end up in a super dog-friendly shop where the staff loves dogs.

They crouch down to fuss over your dog, they offer free treats, and for a brief moment, your dog thinks they're a celebrity.

The worst-case scenario?

Your dog decides this is the perfect moment to pee on a display shelf.

(You will never return to that shop again.)

THE 'SHOULD I BRING MY DOG?' DILEMMA

Now that more places do allow dogs, dog owners face a new question:

"Should I bring them or not?"

Because while it's fun having them with you, there's also the constant risk that something will go wrong.

✓ Best case scenario: Your dog behaves perfectly, and you feel like you've mastered life.

✗ Worst case scenario: Your dog knocks over an entire display stand, you panic, and you leave without buying anything.

Every dog walker has at least one public outing that ended in mild disaster.

- The time your dog stole someone's sandwich at an outdoor café.

- The time they barked at their own reflection in a shop mirror.

- The time they got tangled in a chair leg, causing a domino effect of destruction.

And yet...we keep bringing them.

Because no matter how many awkward encounters we have, there's nothing better than sipping a coffee with your best furry friend sitting right beside you. Even if they do spend the whole time staring at someone else's food.

FINAL CHAPTER:

The Never-Ending Walk

Dog walking is one of those things that never truly ends. Because at the end of the day, walking a dog isn't just about exercise. It's about the moments we share—with our dogs, with strangers, with fellow walkers who know exactly what it's like.

And, most importantly, with the ridiculous, lovable creatures who make every single walk worth it.

For me, that creature is 7.

She doesn't just walk with me—she flies with me. We do a lot together. Whether we're exploring new landscapes together or jetting off to exotic places, she's always by my side, my fearless travel companion. And, of course, when it comes to car journeys, there is no question about seating arrangements—the front seat belongs to her.

7 came into my life as a rescue dog with a broken leg and shoulder—a rough start for a dog built for speed and adventure.

Thanks to the incredible care of my amazing vet, Fay and Nola 'Toll Barn Vets,' she was fixed, healed, and given a second chance to run, jump, and chase every ball in sight.

She follows in the paw prints of some incredible dogs who came before her—Bruno, Alf,

Max, Mazy, Butch, and Softy—each of them a part of my journey, each of them loved beyond measure.

This book is for them, too.

And for all my wonderful dog-walking friends, Barry, Mikita, Glynis, Barbara, and of course, the blond bombshell "Sam," with whom I have shared miles of conversation, countless laughs, and the occasional bag of treats along the way.

Because dog walks don't just bring us closer to our dogs—they bring us closer to people, too.

I should know.

After all, I met Helen on a dog walk. The romance was in the air, even in the depths of mid-winter.
She was dressed for battle, wrapped up in all the right gear. Even in the gloomy morning light, I could see something special beyond the practical layers—a beautiful soul, a beautiful woman and, of course, her two lovely dogs.

So, if there's one thing I've learned from a lifetime of walking dogs, it's this:

You never know what wonderful things can happen on a dog walk.

ABOUT THE AUTHOR

Shaun is a man with a deep heart and a rare gift of seeing what others often overlook. His creativity stems from years as a hairdresser and now an accomplished photographer, so he sees life slightly differently. He finds meaning in the small moments, beauty in the unnoticed, and strength in the unseen. Passionate about life, he embraces its many possibilities, especially those shared with his partner, family, and beloved pet.

In Shaun's world, nothing is impossible. He lives with unshakeable hope and deep faith, always reaching for the light. Even in the darkest places, sometimes that's where we learn to laugh the most.

A believer in second chances and silver linings, looking for the funnier things in life, Shaun finds joy in uncovering the positive in every experience and every person he meets.

His writings reflect a soul that feels deeply, loves life fully, and never stops believing.

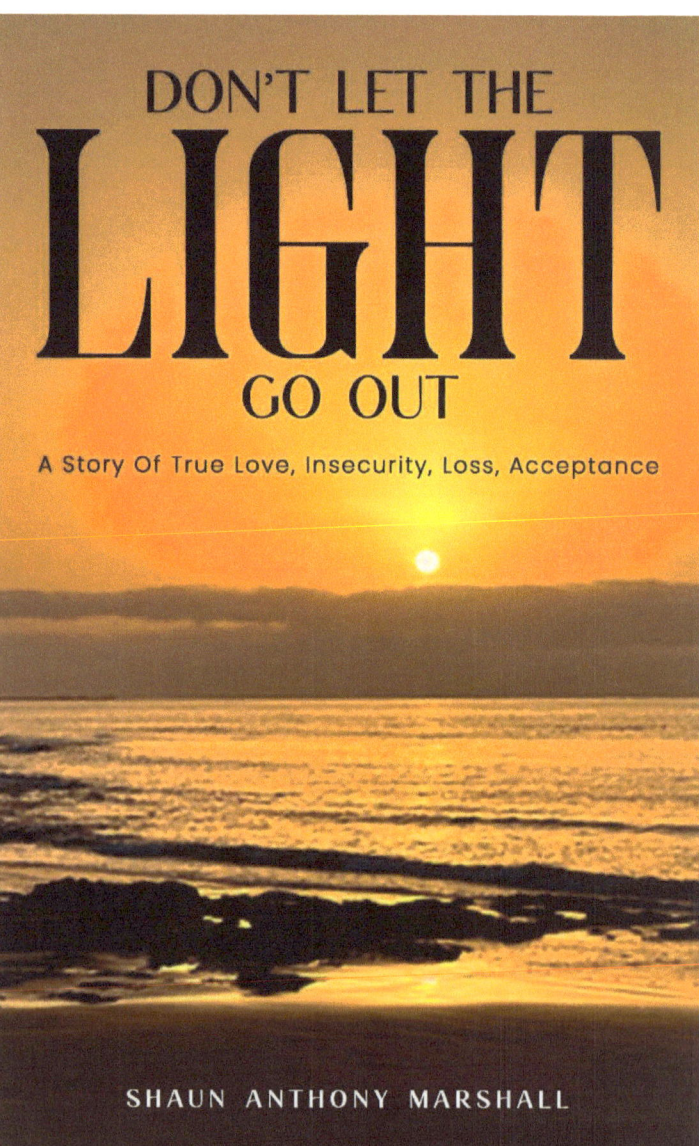

DON'T LET THE

LIGHT

GO OUT

A Story Of True Love, Insecurity, Loss, Acceptance

SHAUN ANTHONY MARSHALL